RIVER FRIENDS

To my sister
Erin Jean
K.M.K.

RIVER FRIENDS

written and illustrated by

Kathleen M. Kelly

ATHENEUM   1988   NEW YORK

One day, a boy named Rusty walked deep into the woods.
He knew of a river on the other side, which he liked to visit
as often as he could.

On one side of the river there was a big rock. The rock looked like a great throne.

From his throne by the river, Rusty listened to the birds. He watched insects darting here and there in the warm sunlight, and saw fish leaping from the water. It seemed that the world belonged to him.

At a particularly quiet time, Rusty noticed a man on top of the hill across the river. "What is he doing here?" Rusty asked himself. He sat very still on his throne.

The stranger moved down the hill. Rusty saw that he was not a man after all, but a boy almost Rusty's size.

The boy came across the river, stood beside Rusty, and
smiled. "My name is Nicholas," he said. Rusty told the boy
his name.

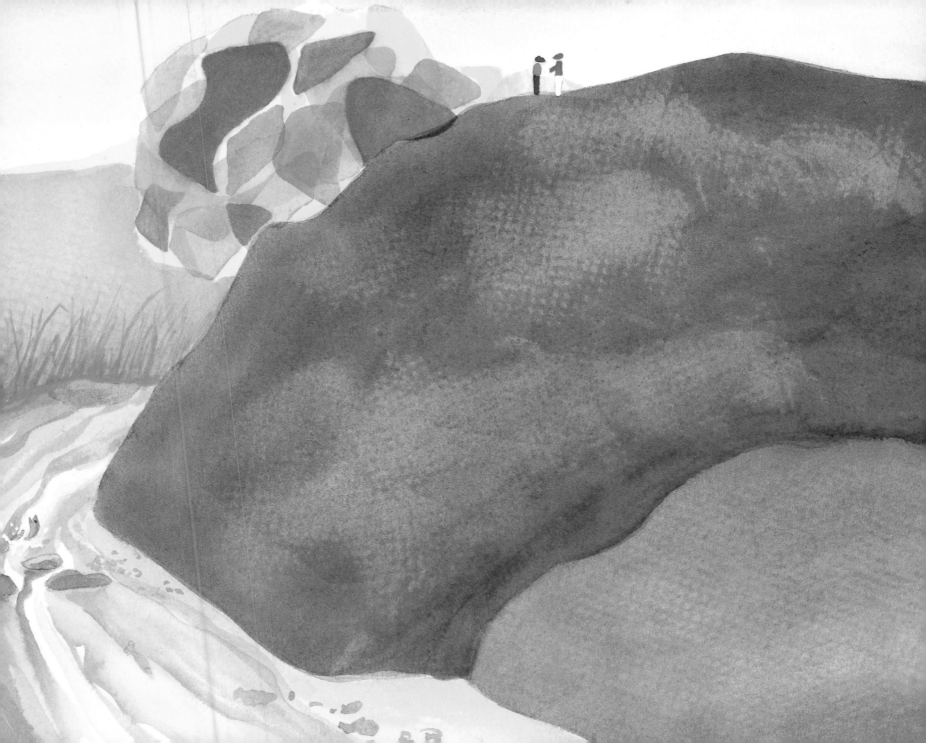

For a while, the two boys sat together on the throne and listened to the river below. Rusty pointed to some birds that dove into the clear water to bathe near the fish. Nicholas also loved to watch the insects darting in the sunlight, and the fish leaping from the water.

Later, Rusty raced Nicholas through the meadow, to the trees
at the forest's edge. Rusty won.

After they had caught their breath, they swam together in the river, jumping off rocks and splashing each other.

In the tall grass at the water's edge, Nicholas found lots of
colored frogs that Rusty had never noticed before.

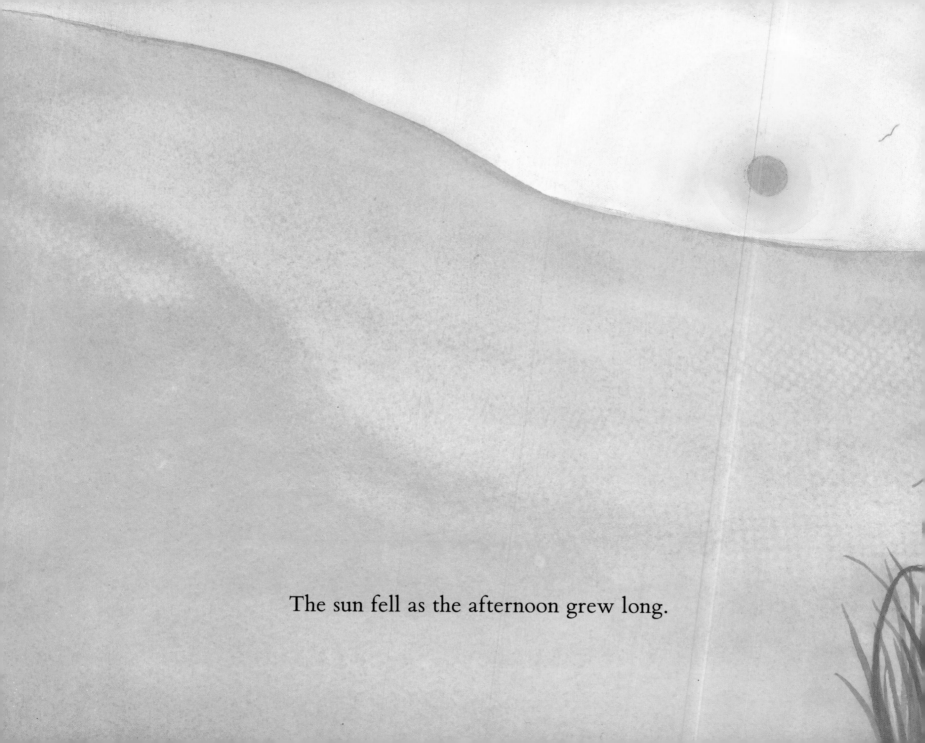

The sun fell as the afternoon grew long.

Rusty said, "I have to leave before the woods get dark."
Nicholas had to leave too. "Let's keep our place a secret,"
he said.

The two boys planned to meet again on the morning of the next sunny day. Nicholas headed for the hilltop, while Rusty climbed the rocky slope and stood on the throne.

There was room enough for two, he decided. In the distance he saw Nicholas waving. Rusty smiled and waved good-bye.

Atheneum
Macmillan Publishing Company
866 Third Avenue, New York, NY 10022
Collier Macmillan Canada, Inc.
First Edition
Printed in Japan
10   9   8   7   6   5   4   3   2   1

Library of Congress Cataloging-in-Publication Data
Kelly, Kathleen M.
River friends.
Summary: Rusty meets a new friend at the river and
decides he can, after all, share what he once felt
belonged only to him.
[1. Sharing—Fiction.   2. Friendship—Fiction]
I. Title
PZ7.K29635Ri   1988   [E]   87-35140
ISBN 0-689-31412-4